T0413469

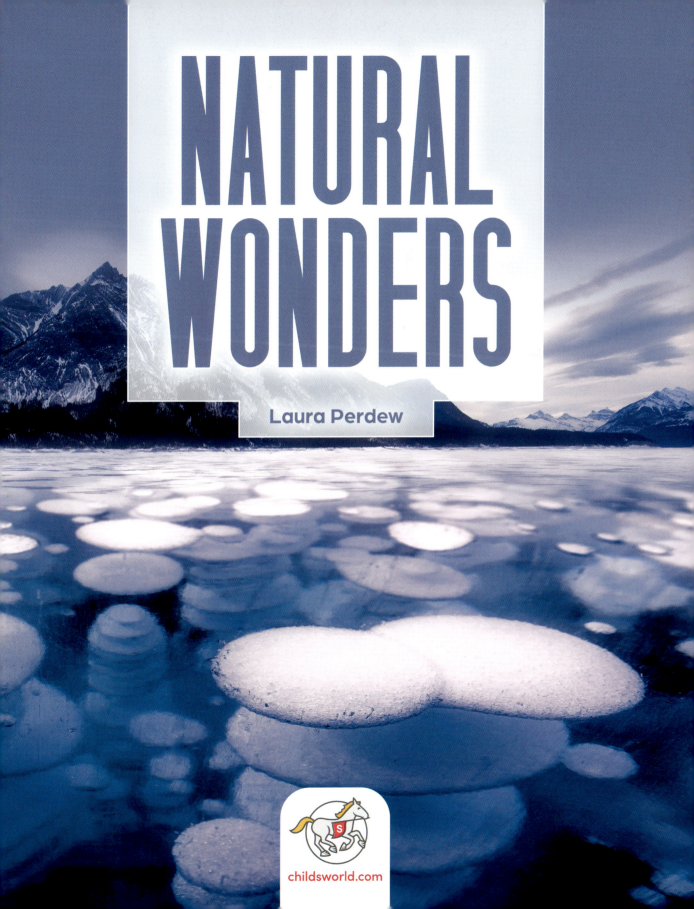

NATURAL WONDERS

Laura Perdew

childsworld.com

Published by The Child's World®

800-599-READ • www.childsworld.com

Photography Credits

Photographs ©: Shutterstock Images, cover, 1, 6, 9, 10; Christopher Moswitzer/Shutterstock Images, 2–3; Tilpunov Mikhail/Shutterstock Images, 5; Jim Peaco/National Park Service, 12; Lauren Dauphin/NASA, 13; Paul Brady Photography/Shutterstock Images, 15; Anatoliy Lukich/Shutterstock Images, 16; Alexander Piragis/Shutterstock Images, 19; Red Line Editorial, 20; Miguel Angel/Shutterstock Images, 21

ISBN Information

9781503894464 (Reinforced Library Binding)
9781503895195 (Portable Document Format)
9781503896017 (Online Multi-user eBook)
9781503896833 (Electronic Publication)

LCCN 2024942896

Printed in the United States of America

ABOUT THE AUTHOR

Laura Perdew is an author coach, presenter, former teacher, and the author of more than 60 fiction and nonfiction books for kids. Her books highlight the wonders of nature and the environment and call for action to preserve them. She lives in Boulder, Colorado.

CONTENTS

CHAPTER ONE

FROZEN ICE BUBBLES

People look through the clear ice of a frozen lake. Below the surface, there are hundreds and hundreds of frozen bubbles. The white, curvy blobs are different shapes and sizes. They seem to hang in the frozen water. They are stacked on top of each other. Some even look like a pile of pancakes. They polka-dot the lake.

METHANE

The frozen bubbles are a natural wonder. They are also dangerous when the lake melts. The gas bubbles are released. They fizz and pop. The popping bubbles release the methane inside. The gas is very flammable. It is also a **greenhouse gas** that contributes to **climate change**.

The trapped bubbles have risen from the bottom of the lake. They are not filled with air. The frozen bubbles are made of **methane**.

This natural wonder started long before the lake froze. It started with dead plants and animals that ended up in the lake. The decaying matter sank to the bottom. There, the matter began to break down.

Lake Baikal in Russia is the oldest and deepest lake in the world. It is also a place where people can see frozen methane bubbles.

Abraham Lake is in the Rocky Mountains.

Microbes ate the matter and released methane gas. The gas floated toward the water's surface in bubbles. But the gas bubbles became trapped in the frozen water.

Abraham Lake in Alberta, Canada, is famous for its frozen bubbles. There are bubbles all across the lake in the winter. A road runs alongside the western shore. There are rest stops along the road where people can stop to view the bubbles. The best time to see them is between mid-January and February.

Frozen bubbles occur in other places, too. There are many lakes in the Canadian Rocky Mountains that have them. Other lakes across the Arctic have frozen bubbles. They also occur in the Arctic Ocean near Siberia. Scientists found a huge bubble there that was more than a half mile (900 m) wide!

The world is filled with natural wonders. Methane bubbles are just one example. Colorful lakes, sailing stones, and lenticular clouds are others. These weird and wacky occurrences can all be explained by science.

CHAPTER TWO

COLORFUL LAKES

Lakes are found all over the world. They come in all shapes and sizes. Some are shallow, and others are deep. They also come in many different colors. Water itself is not colorful. But the things inside a lake can give it color.

Minerals and dissolved metals in the water can affect a lake's color. So can water temperature, **sulfur**, the water's salt level, and rock or sand particles in the water. Some algae and other microorganisms thrive in these environments. They can also affect the water color.

In Western Australia, there are several lakes the color of bubble gum. Lake Hillier is one of the best-known pink lakes. The lake is 2,000 feet (600 m) long and stands out against the green forest around it. The lake is very salty. It is even saltier than the ocean! Scientists discovered algae, bacteria, and other microbes thriving in the lake.

Lake Hillier is hard to get to. People usually take a helicopter tour to see it.

Purple and red microbes turn the lake pink. The water is not dangerous to people. But because it is so salty, people should not drink it.

Other pink lakes change color depending on the water temperature. But Lake Hillier stays the same bright pink all the time. The water still looks pink even when put in a bottle.

New Zealand's tallest mountain, called Aoraki or Mount Cook, can be seen from Lake Pukaki.

Lake Pukaki in New Zealand is another colorful lake. The turquoise lake is 9.5 miles (15 km) long. It is 5 miles (8 km) wide. Mountains surround the lake. Nearby glaciers are responsible for the lake's color.

Glaciers are slow-moving masses of ice formed on land. As they move, they grind and push rock through valleys like bulldozers. The grinding breaks down the rock. It turns it into a fine **silt** called glacial flour. As glaciers near Lake Pukaki melt, the water carries the glacial flour into the lake. It is so fine that it does not sink to the bottom. Instead, it hangs in the water. There, the water absorbs blue and purple light. This causes the lake to look bright blue to human eyes.

Lake Pukaki is not the only turquoise lake caused by glacial flour. There are several others near Lake Pukaki, including Lake Tekapo. Peyto Lake and Lake Louise are turquoise lakes in Canada.

Kawah Ijen Lake in Indonesia is bright blue, similar to Lake Pukaki. However, that lake's color does not come from glacial flour. Kawah Ijen Lake sits in a volcanic crater. Sulfur from the volcano mixes with dissolved metals in the lake to give the water its vibrant hue.

Grand Prismatic Spring is in Yellowstone National Park. A rainbow-colored ring at its edges comes from bacteria that thrive in hot water. Green Lake in Austria gets its deep green color from a mix of factors. These include green algae and the pure, clear water from snowmelt. Finely crushed rock particles also hang in the water, reflecting blue-green light.

Yellowstone National Park is in Wyoming, Montana, and Idaho. The Grand Prismatic Spring is in Wyoming.

The Kelimutu lakes can change color suddenly.

Mount Kelimutu is a volcano near Flores, Indonesia. There are three crater lakes at the top of the volcano. Each one is a different color, and the colors can change. The lakes have appeared blue, white, red, brown, green, and even black. Scientists think the colors are caused by minerals in the water mixing with gases from the volcano. These are only some of the many colorful lakes around the world.

CHAPTER THREE

SAILING STONES

Death Valley National Park sits on the border between California and Nevada. It is one of the driest and hottest places on Earth. Death Valley is also home to a natural wonder. There are stones there that seem to move on their own.

The sailing stones leave well-defined tracks behind them on the ground, as if they were dragged. Some of the tracks are hundreds of feet long. Some tracks are curved. Others follow a straight path, then curve to the side. In addition, the stones often sit for years without moving.

For a long time, how the stones moved remained a mystery. No one had ever seen the stones moving. There were many guesses. Some people suggested that aliens or **dust devils** were responsible. Others guessed that **magnetic fields** moved the stones.

The cause of Death Valley's sailing stones was a mystery for many years.

Sailing stones can move in straight or curved paths. Some change direction.

Scientists began researching the mystery in the 1940s. It was finally solved in 2014. The stones move due to a combination of several weather conditions, including temperature, water, wind, and ice.

First, it must rain several inches, which is rare in that region. Water fills the **playa** a few inches deep. At night, the temperature drops. The water freezes into thin ice sheets.

In the morning, warming temperatures break the ice into panes that float on the water. When the wind blows, the panes knock up against the stones. This moves the stones across the muddy bottom.

The ice must be thick enough to move the stones yet thin enough to float freely. After the playa dries up, all that remains are the moved stones and the paths they left.

People can see the sailing stones for themselves. The stones are found in a dry lake bed called Racetrack Playa. This is in a remote part of Death Valley National Park. It can be reached by car, but people must be aware of changing road conditions. Many cars cannot handle the dangerous roads. Vehicles with good tires and plenty of distance from the ground are recommended.

THE STONE'S PATH

The sailing stones vary in size and shape. Some weigh as much as 700 pounds (320 kg). They vary in texture, too. A stone's texture can determine the path it takes. Straight tracks are left by stones with rough bottoms. A smoother stone leaves a curved track.

CHAPTER FOUR

LENTICULAR CLOUDS

Sometimes clouds form in the shape of discs or shallow, upside–down bowls. There may be several stacked on top of each other, like pancakes in the sky. These are lenticular clouds. Because of their shape, some people believe they look like UFOs. But these flying saucer–like clouds are not from outer space. They are the result of normal weather events right here on Earth. They form when wind carrying moisture moves up and over a mountain. As the wind hits the mountain, it forms a wave. At the same time, the rising air cools. The water vapor in the air **condenses**, and a cloud forms at the **crest** of the wave, making the mountain look like it is wearing a cap.

Lenticular clouds may look like a hat or a blanket formed over a mountain.

Other clouds continually drift across the sky. Lenticular clouds do not. Instead, they look like they are hovering in place. But the cloud is not actually still. It is evaporating on the downside of the wave as the air warms and dries. As cool air continues to flow, the cloud is constantly reforming on the front side. This gives the illusion that the cloud stays in place. Lenticular clouds can stay in one place for several hours.

HOW LENTICULAR CLOUDS FORM

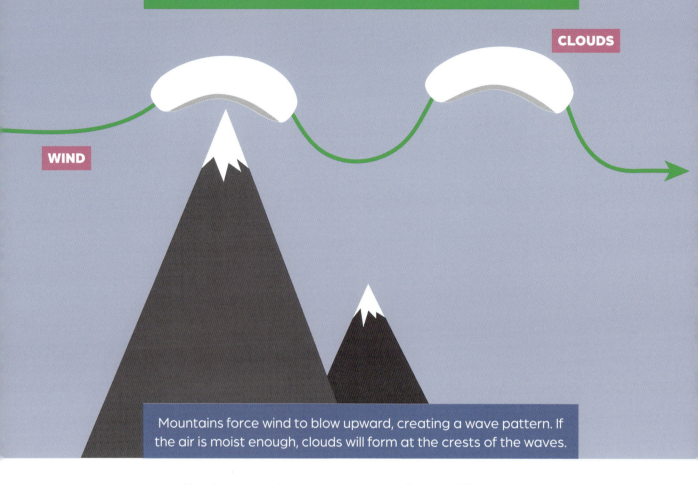

CLOUDS

WIND

Mountains force wind to blow upward, creating a wave pattern. If the air is moist enough, clouds will form at the crests of the waves.

Lenticular clouds can be seen all over. They are most common near mountains and hills, but they can even appear over tall buildings. While they can occur at any time of day, the best time to view lenticular clouds is at sunrise or sunset. Low sunlight offers color and contrast to the clouds. They are also more easily viewed when the rest of the sky is clear.

Lenticular clouds are not the only interesting clouds people might see. And there are many other natural wonders, too. From funky clouds to stunning lakes, Earth is full of mysterious natural beauty. People who observe the world around them may be lucky enough to see these wonders for themselves!

Lenticular clouds can stack up like pancakes.

GLOSSARY

climate change (KLYE-mut CHAYNJ) Climate change is the change in Earth's long-term temperature and weather patterns. Methane contributes to climate change.

condenses (kun-DEN-sez) When a substance condenses, it changes from vapor or gas to liquid. As water vapor condenses, it forms clouds.

crest (KREST) The crest is the highest point or top of something. A lenticular cloud sometimes forms at the crest of a wave of air as it passes over a mountain or hill.

dust devils (DUST DEH-vuhlz) Dust devils are powerful whirlwinds that gather loose soil into a funnel. Some people believed that dust devils moved the sailing stones in Death Valley.

greenhouse gas (GREEN-howss GAS) A greenhouse gas is a type of gas that traps warm air near Earth, similar to how greenhouses keep air warm for plants. Methane is a greenhouse gas that contributes to climate change.

magnetic fields (mag-NET-ik FEELDZ) Magnetic fields are invisible forces that attract certain types of metals. Some people believed that magnetic fields were responsible for moving Death Valley's sailing stones.

methane (METH-ayn) Methane is an odorless, colorless gas. The frozen bubbles in Arctic lakes are filled with methane.

microbes (MY-krohbz) Microbes are tiny organisms that are too small to be seen with the naked eye. Microbes that ate decaying matter at the bottom of Abraham Lake released methane bubbles.

playa (PLY-uh) A playa is a dry lake bed, often in a desert basin. Racetrack Playa is well known for its sailing stones.

silt (SILT) Silt is made up of fine particles of soil or rock that are carried by moving water and eventually settle in a lake or river. Silt in a lake can cause the water to appear bright blue.

sulfur (SUHL-fer) Sulfur is a natural chemical element. Volcanoes often release sulfur.

FAST FACTS

✳ Ice bubbles form when methane bubbles get trapped in frozen water.

✳ Lake Hillier in Australia is bubblegum pink because of the purple and red microbes living in it.

✳ In New Zealand, Lake Pukaki appears turquoise blue to the human eye because of glacial flour in the water.

✳ Kawah Ijen Lake in Indonesia gets its bright-blue color from a mix of sulfur and dissolved metals.

✳ Three lakes at the top of Mount Kelimutu in Indonesia each change color. Scientists think this happens when gases from the volcano mix with minerals in the water.

✳ Sailing stones are moved by sheets of ice floating in the shallow basin of Racetrack Playa, leaving tracks behind them in the muddy desert soil.

✳ Lenticular clouds are shaped like flying saucers. They form over mountains when wind and moisture conditions are just right.

ONE STRIDE FURTHER

✳ Why do you think people are fascinated by ice bubbles?

✳ Which colorful lake would you like to visit? Why?

✳ Why do you think it took scientists so long to solve the mystery of the sailing stones?

✳ Where do you think you could go to see lenticular clouds near you?

FIND OUT MORE

IN THE LIBRARY

Allen, Stacy. *Rainbows and Halos*. Parker, CO: The Child's World, 2025.

Leighton, Abby. *National Parks Maps*. Layton, UT: Gibbs Smith, 2021.

Ralston, Fraser and Judith Ralston. *What's the Weather?* New York, NY: DK Publishing, 2021.

ON THE WEB

Visit our website for links about natural wonders:

childsworld.com/links

Note to Parents, Caregivers, Teachers, and Librarians: We routinely verify our web links to make sure they are safe and active sites. So encourage your readers to check them out!

INDEX